Personal, Social and Health Education

TIME TO TALK

BOOK 2
for ages 5/6

Jim Green

CollinsEducational

Published by Collins Educational, 77-85 Fulham Palace Road, London W6 8JB An imprint of HarperCollins*Publishers*

ISBN 0 00 3187918

Commissioning editor
Graham Bradbury

Edited by
Paula Hammond

Series consultant
Mary Coulthurst, Oxhey Infant School, Hertfordshire

Production by
Angela Davies

Design and page layout by
Carla Turchini

Illustrated by
Helen Herbert
Maureen Carter

Printed and bound at Redwood Books, Trowbridge, Wiltshire

Contents

Contents of the three **Time to Talk** books

Book 

Book 

I am growing
GROWING AND CHANGING

I can play
CO-OPERATION

When I started school
SHARING MEMORIES

Let me tell you
COMMUNICATION

Eating and drinking
IMPORTANCE OF FOOD

Happy and sad
HANDLING EMOTIONS

Invitations
TIMES OF CELEBRATION

Family outings
COMMUNICATION SKILLS

Helping and hurting
PERSONAL RELATIONSHIPS

When I am ill
CARE IN ILLNESS

Good and bad
MAKING JUDGEMENTS

Come and visit
ORGANIZATION SKILLS

The clinic
LOCAL HEALTH CARE ENVIRONMENT

My school
THE SCHOOL ENVIRONMENT

Places I like to visit
THE WIDER ENVIRONMENT

People I see
PEOPLE IN THE COMMUNITY

Busy places
SERVICES IN THE COMMUNITY

Quiet places
THE SOUND ENVIRONMENT

Book 

Yes and no
RESPONSIBLE CHOICES

Right and wrong
MORAL JUDGEMENTS

When I started school
CHANGING AND GROWING

Look what I can do
DEVELOPING SKILLS

When you are as old as me
AGEING

I am changing
THE MATURING PROCESS

Me and my family
FAMILY MEMBERSHIP

Goodbye
COPING WITH LOSS

Let's celebrate
TIMES OF CELEBRATION

Who looks after me?
CARERS

Happy and sad
FRIENDSHIP

Telling the truth
HONESTY

Things that belong to us all
THE COMMUNITY ENVIRONMENT

Am I safe?
PERSONAL SAFETY

Getting around
TRANSPORT AND MOBILITY

After school
HOME PASTIMES

Where I live
UNDERSTANDING THE LOCAL ENVIRONMENT

I wish we had
LOCAL AMENITIES

Time to Talk

INTRODUCTION

This book is made up of three themes: **Myself**, **My Family and Friends** and **Where I Live**. These themes are designed to help you to promote personal and social awareness in children – to help them develop a sense of their own identity and place it in the context of who they meet and where they live.

The material in this book provides learning activities which place before children, in an appropriate way, some of the issues which are central to healthy growth and development. By using *Time to Talk* it is hoped that the children will be encouraged to become aware of their own and others' physical identity and will grow in an understanding of their own uniqueness and the uniqueness of others. This building of a sense of self-identity will be complemented by exploring how we share so much with others and they with us, thus forming the basis of a sense of community.

Each of the three themes contains six 'lessons' which deal with a specific area of Personal, Social and Health Education. The time needed for each 'lesson' will vary according to individual needs and circumstances.

MANAGEMENT NOTES

Each lesson contains a full page of management notes, which are meant as guidelines on how the lesson might be developed. Within the management notes teachers will find guidance on:

Preparation

Preparation sets out details of what needs to be done, in advance, to prepare for the lesson.

Discussion

In each case the *Discussion* notes give examples of points worth bringing out during the discussion, as well as suggested possible strategies to use – questions to raise with the children, or ideas for activities that tie-in with the topic of discussion. However, the suggested questions are only meant to illustrate *one* of the ways discussion of the topic might go. Discussion is best directed and controlled but should never be made rigid and inflexible, as talk is often a time for expression, exploration and learning from one another.

It is assumed that in this area of the curriculum, particularly, discussion is vital. The children should, therefore, gather for discussion in a way that is orderly but friendly and that will encourage them to learn to talk, listen, respond and take turns.

Follow-up activity

The notes on the *Follow-up activity* are meant to explain and expand on work on the 'activity copymaster' (see below).

COPYMASTERS

Each lesson also includes three photocopiable 'copymasters':

Follow-up activity copymaster

The first copymaster is intended to be a practical activity which will reinforce and develop the theme of the particular lesson. A follow-up activity copymaster is provided for each lesson, although there could be many activities to follow up discussions, and the one provided can be replaced with something more appropriate if you so wish.

Song/poem/story/game copymaster

Children love songs, poems, stories and games - and one of these is provided for each lesson. These sheets are designed to be photocopied and can be used in a variety of ways – for example, they can be coloured in by the children, used in class, taken home, or enlarged as part of a classroom display.

Where songs are provided they can be sung to well-known tunes or chanted to a steady rhythm. They need no special musical skills. Sometimes the songs and poems encourage actions to be used with the words. These actions are generally illustrated on the copymaster so that, even if children can not read the words they and others (should they take the sheets home) can see what they are required to do.

In general the song, poem, story or game copymaster will be self explanatory. Occasionally, however, extra guidance or ideas to expand on the copymaster will be given in the management notes.

Can you help? copymaster

The *Can you help? copymasters* are for use in a one-to-one situation, if this can be arranged. Personal and social development must seek to be centred on the individual. Children desperately need to talk and be listened to as individuals. However, it is not always practical or desirable for the teacher to do all the talking and listening. These copymasters are designed, therefore, to be used both in and out of school. Sometimes they will be best used at home, sometimes in school with the teacher, another adult or an older child. They can form a vital link with parents. However, the situation of each school and each household is so different that the copymasters are designed to be suitably varied and flexible, for as many situations as possible.

It is hoped that *Time to Talk* will support teachers in placing before children rich and appropriate learning activities. It is a resource to develop, change, adapt and build on. In using *Time to Talk* we hope you will see children grow and develop, both as healthy individuals, and as members of their communities.

1

I am growing

GROWING AND CHANGING

Aims

- to help children to understand that people change as they get older.
- to explain how everybody continues to change - even when they have stopped growing physically.

Preparation

Before the lesson, send home photocopies of the **Can you help? copymaster** for discussion between the child and parent/guardian.

Assemble a collection of photos of yourself (or some other adult well known to the children). Ideally these photos should show a progression from the time when you were very young, to the age you are now. The children will also be asked to bring in a photograph of themselves when they were very little (see the **Can you help? copymaster**). Mount the photos (ensuring the mounts can be easily removed without damaging the photos) and display them under the heading "I am growing". This display can either be a wall display or a large book.

Make enough copies of the **I am growing copymaster** so that all the children can have one each.

Make copies of **The missing words poem**, as necessary.

Discussion

Points to bring out

- We are all growing.
- When you stop growing you still get older and still change.

Strategies to try

If the facilities are available, copy and enlarge a selection of the photographs that have been brought in. (Black and white photos will work better than colour.)

Tell the children that they are going to look at photos of members of the class. Tell them that, if their photo is shown, they mustn't say anything because the rest of the class have to guess who is in the photo.

When they have had a go at guessing which of their classmates were in the photos that you showed them, hold up one of the photos of yourself (as a baby, if possible). If they guess who the photo is of, go on to show the other photos of yourself. Tell the children that they are going to look at how you have grown. Can they guess your age in each photo?

Follow-up activity

Hand out copies of the **I am growing copymaster**. Ask the children to draw a figure in each of the empty modes of transport.

Which one could be you?

Poem

The missing words poem is fun just before morning break, and can be used to either end or begin the discussion on 'growing'. Ask the children to help you to fill in the missing words in the last lines of each verse.

I am growing

Here are some ways of getting around.
Draw someone in each one.
Can you write who is in each picture?

The missing words poem

Can you find the words that fit the spaces?

First you are a baby,
Very very small.
You cannot walk, you cannot run,
And so you have to _________ .

Next you are a toddler,
Learning how to talk.
You cannot run, you cannot skip,
And so you have to _________ .

When you go to playschool,
You play and you have fun.
When mummy comes to get you,
Out you _________ .

Now that you are older,
You go to school each day.
And when the break at morning comes,
You all go out to _________ .

[Affix school letterhead if required]

Dear Parent/Guardian,

Can you help?
In preparation for a lesson we are having it would be very helpful if you could read this letter from your child.

I am growing

At school we are going to share with each other memories about when we were very young, as part of our lesson called "I am growing".

Please could you spend some time looking at photos of me when I was very little and tell me a little bit about when the photos were taken and where?

Please would you chose one of the photos we have been looking at and let me take it to school? I will bring it back safely when I have finished with it.

Thank you for helping me,

Myself

2

I can play

CO-OPERATION

Aims

- to help children to realize that, for a game to be fun, everyone must work together and follow the rules.
- to lead children on to learn, through play, the importance of co-operation.

Preparation

Bring in a selection of table games that the children can play in groups. These could be board games or games that the children play regularly in class. The games should be ones that involve taking turns and working together. It would help the discussion if the children could have played the game on the **I can play copymaster** before the lesson.

Make copies of the **I can play copymaster**, as necessary.

Make copies of **The frog game** – one for every pair of children. Make sure that cardboard, glue, scissors and dice are available to help the children make and play the game.

As a follow-up to work done during this lesson you may want to send home photocopies of the **Can you help? copymaster** for discussion between the child and parent/guardian.

TIME TO TALK

Dear Parent/Guardian,

Can you help?
As a follow-up to work that we have recently done in school it would be helpful if you could read this letter from your child.

I can play

At school we have had a lesson about the games that we can play together

- Will you tell me about some of the games that we play together at home?
- Do any of the games we play at home have rules?
- Is it important to have rules in a game? Why?
- Will you teach me a new game that I can play at home with you?

Thank you for helping me.

Discussion

Points to bring out

- Games are fun.
- There are lots of games to play and lots more to learn.
- We can play games at school or at home.
- Games are more fun if everybody has a good time.

Strategies to try

Begin by making a list of actions that can reasonably be attempted by the children in the class (e.g., stand on one leg, dance, pretend to be a frog, etc.). The children then sit in a circle. One child skips round the outside of the circle while the rest of the class sing the song from the **I can play copymaster**. When the song ends the child stops. Whoever they have stopped behind has to stand in the circle and perform one of the actions from the list that you made. The game is over when no more children can fit into the circle.

Continue with a discussion:

The way you play a game is called having rules. These tell you how to play.
Do you know any other games we can play? (*You might like to make a list on A3 paper or on the board.*)
Are there any games which we all know?
Can we make a list of the rules of this game?

Games are fun. They are happy ways to spend time with our friends or family. Would it be a good game if it made someone sad?

Follow-up activity

Hand out copies of **The frog game** – one for every pair of children. Ask them to colour in the game, stick it on to card and cut it out. The children must then work together to decide on the rules for the game. For example:
What happens on a 'hop' square?
Who goes first?
Who is the winner?

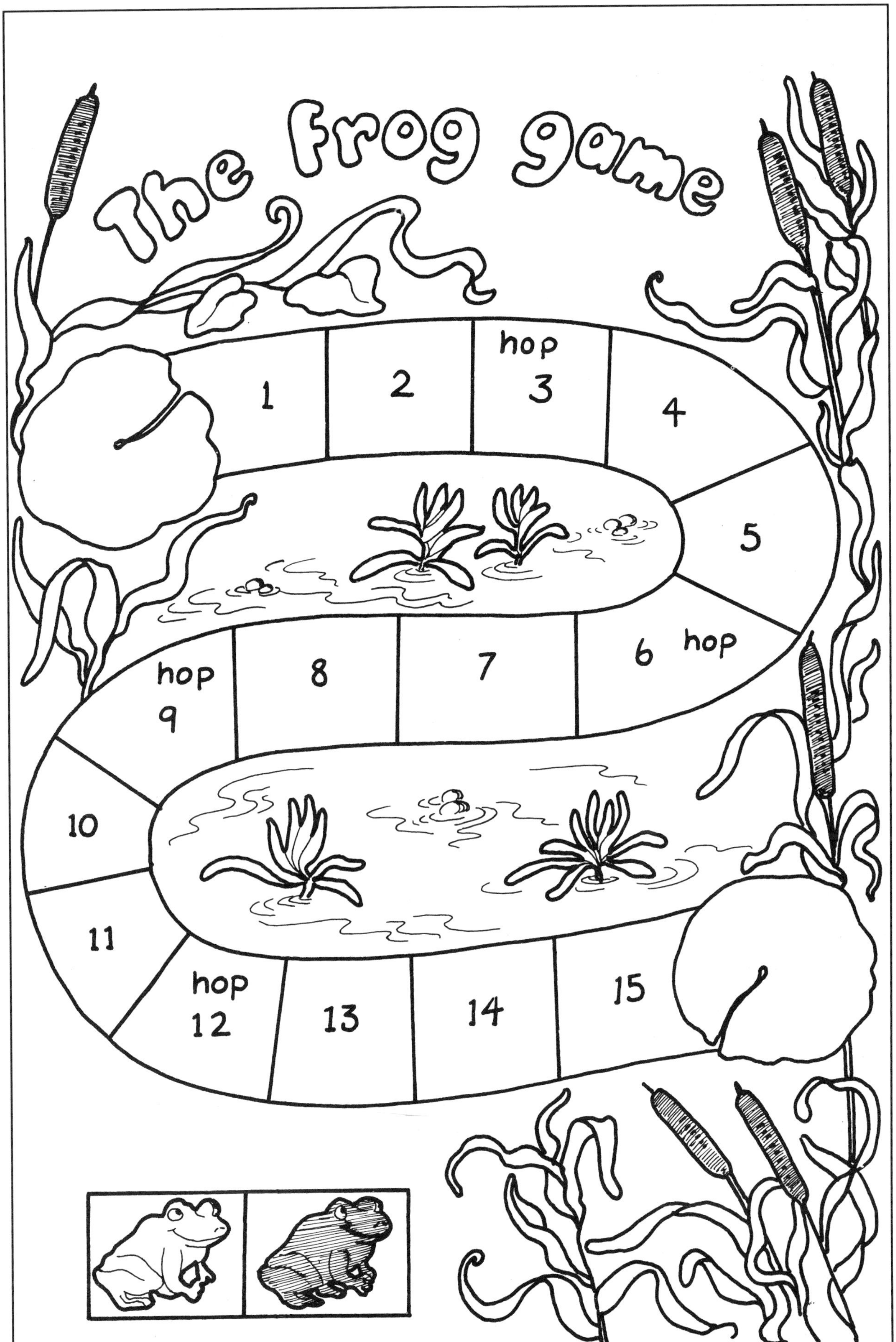

The frog game

1	2	hop 3	4	5	6 hop	7	8	hop 9	10	11	hop 12	13	14	15

I can play

(A singing game played to the tune of "Nick Nack Paddy Wack".)

I can shout,
I can sing,
I can do so many things.
Wash my hands,
And my face too,
Now let's see what you can do.

[Affix school letterhead if required]

Dear Parent/Guardian,

Can you help?
As a follow-up to work that we have recently done in school it would be helpful if you could read this letter from your child.

I can play

At school we have had a lesson about the games that we can play together.

- Will you tell me about some of the games that we play together at home?
- Do any of the games we play at home have rules?
- Is it important to have rules in a game? Why?
- Will you teach me a new game that I can play at home with you?

Thank you for helping me,

3

When I started school

SHARING MEMORIES

Aim

▶ to teach children the value of memories and of sharing memories with others.

Preparation

Before the lesson, send home photocopies of the **Can you help? copymaster** for discussion between the child and parent/guardian.

Ask the teacher of the reception class whether there is a mum or dad who could talk to the children and answer questions about their child's first day at school.

Make enough copies of the **My first day at school copymaster** so that all the children can have one each.

Make copies of the **Starting school poem**, as necessary.

TIME TO TALK

Starting school

I remember, I remember,
When I first came to school,
The children and the teachers
And the most important rule

I remember, I remember,
The rule we had to know,
We had to leave our mums and dads
We had to let them go

I remember, I remember,
How I began to cry,
When all the mums and dads had gone,
And I had said "goodbye"

I remember, I remember,
How the teacher helped us play,
And how I found some nice new friends,
And how I loved the day

I remember, I remember,
When all the day had gone
How with a smile and piece of work,
I ran out to my mum

I remember, I remember,
That day so long ago,
And now I have a little boy
Who soon will have to go

I remember, I remember,
That he'll now learn the rule,
To say goodbye and watch me go,
And start his life at school

Discussion

Points to bring out

- Memories are like stories, but they are special because they are true.

Strategies to try

Introduce the visitor and explain that they are going to share with us what they remember about their child's first day at school.

Ask the visitor:

Were you worried about the first day?
Did you do anything special at home to get ready?
Was your child looking forward to starting school?
What happened when you got to school?
How did you feel when you had to leave?
Did you think about your child during the day?
Did the mums and dads talk to each other while they were waiting at the end of the day?
What did your child say about their first day?
Do you think you will remember that first day for a long time?
Are memories like this important to you? Tell us why.

The children can be encouraged to ask their own questions as the discussion develops.

Follow-up activity

Hand out copies of the **My first day at school copymaster** and ask the children to colour in the picture of themselves waving goodbye to their parents/guardians on their first day at school. Ask them to write "This is me. This is my mum/dad".

Poem

Read the children the **Starting school poem**.

What was that poem all about?
Is the person in the poem a child?
How can you tell?

My first day at school

Who are you waving "goodbye" to?

Starting school

I remember, I remember,
When I first came to school,
The children and the teachers,
And the most important rule.

I remember, I remember,
The rule we had to know,
We had to leave our mums and dads,
We had to let them go.

I remember, I remember,
How I began to cry,
When all the mums and dads had gone,
And I had said "goodbye".

I remember, I remember,
How the teacher helped us play,
And how I found some nice new friends,
And how I loved the day.

I remember, I remember,
When all the day had gone,
How with a smile and piece of work,
I ran out to my mum.

I remember, I remember,
That day so long ago,
And now I have a little boy,
Who soon will have to go.

I remember, I remember,
That he'll now learn the rule,
To say goodbye and watch me go,
And start his life at school.

[Affix school letterhead if required]

Dear Parent/Guardian,

Can you help?
In preparation for a lesson we are having it would be very helpful if you could read this letter from your child.

When I started school

At school we are having a lesson called "When I started school".

Please could you tell me:

- Do you remember your first day at school?
- Do you remember how you felt?
- Can you remember what you did?
- Who was your teacher?
- What was the best thing about your first day at school?
- Was there anything that upset you on your first day at school?

Thank you for helping me,

4

Let me tell you

COMMUNICATION

Aim

- to introduce children to simple letter writing skills.

Preparation

Before the lesson, send home photocopies of the **Can you help? copymaster** for discussion between the child and parent/guardian.

Have an envelope for each child. Cut sheets of plain paper into strips, and write the names of the children in your class clearly – one on each strip. If there is an odd number of pieces of paper include your own name. Make a class 'post box'. [N.B. Receiving the letters the children send in this lesson will provide the initial activity of **Lesson 6 – Happy and sad**. When planning your lessons, therefore, it is important to try to make sure that the time between this lesson and **Happy and sad** is not too long.]

Make copies of the **My letter copymaster** so that all the children can have one each.

Make copies of **The letter song**, as necessary.

TIME TO TALK

The letter song

(A song sung to the tune of "Here We Go Round The Mulberry Bush")

Can you do the action to this song?

This is how we write a letter,
write a letter,
write a letter.
This is how we write a letter,
Early in the morning

This is how we stick the stamp,
stick the stamp,
stick the stamp,
This is how we stick the stamp,
Early in the morning

This is how we post the letter,
post the letter,
post the letter,
This is how we post the letter,
Early in the morning

This is how we read the letter,
read the letter,
read the letter,
This is how we read the letter,
Early in the morning

This is how we tell our friends,
tell our friends,
tell our friends,
This is how we tell our friends,
Early in the morning

22

Discussion

Points to bring out

- It is nice to get letters.
- We are more likely to get letters if we send some.
- Letters are one way of keeping in touch and of telling friends and family our news.

Strategies to try

Begin with a discussion about what letters (and cards) people get and about the special times when people get lots of post.

Then, explain that we are going to write letters and be given the name of someone in the class to send them to. Hand out copies of the **My letter copymaster** and go through it with the children, suggesting ideas of things that might go into their letters.

Follow-up activity

Hand out the sheets of paper with the names on - one to each child. Ask the children to fill in the **My letter copymaster**. (This can be done in whatever combination of writing and pictures is most suited to the ability of the child.)

Then give each child an envelope and ask them to write/copy the name from the sheet of paper on to the front of the envelope. When they have finished the letter and put it in the envelope they can 'post' it in the class post box.

Song

Sing **The letter song** with the children and encourage them to learn the actions.

Further verses could include: "This is how the letter arrives" and "This is how we open the letter".

Can the children think of any actions to go with these verses?

My letter

Dear Friend,

The thing I like best at school is

The thing I don't like at school is

From,

The letter song

(A song sung to the tune of "Here We Go Round The Mulberry Bush".)

This is how we write a letter,
write a letter,
write a letter,
This is how we write a letter,
Early in the morning.

Can you do the action to this song?

This is how we stick the stamp,
stick the stamp,
stick the stamp,
This is how we stick the stamp,
Early in the morning.

This is how we post the letter,
post the letter,
post the letter,
This is how we post the letter,
Early in the morning.

This is how we read the letter,
read the letter,
read the letter,
This is how we read the letter,
Early in the morning.

This is how we tell our friends,
tell our friends,
tell our friends,
This is how we tell our friends,
Early in the morning.

[Affix school letterhead if required]

Dear Parent/Guardian,

Can you help?
In preparation for a lesson we are having it would be very helpful if you could read this letter from your child.

Let me tell you

At school I am going to write a letter and send it to my friend. It will be about the things that I like best at school and the things that I don't like at school.

- Do you ever write letters?
- Who do you write to?
- Would you like to get a letter from someone?
- Will you help me to choose someone to write a real letter to?
- Will you help me write my letter and post it?

Thank you for helping me,

5 Eating and drinking

IMPORTANCE OF FOOD

Aims

- to help children to understand why we need food.
- to explain how the body processes the food we eat.
- to make it clear that, to stay well, we need to eat good food and a well balanced diet.

Preparation

Before the lesson, send home photocopies of the **Can you help? copymaster** for discussion between the child and the parent/guardian.

Cut out some pictures of cars, vans, lorries, etc from magazines, newspapers, etc.

Cut out some pictures of different foods and drinks.

Make enough copies of the **I can feed myself copymaster** so that every child can have a copy to work on. If possible, make an A3 copy of the sheet to refer to during the class discussion.

Make copies of the **Nora's cake story**, as necessary.

Discussion

Points to bring out

- We get our energy from food.
- For food to keep us healthy it must be clean, fresh and well kept.
- Bad food makes us ill.

Strategies to try

Things that work, like engines in cars, need something to keep them working. What do all these need? (*Hold up the pictures of the cars, etc.*)

Cars need energy – which they get from petrol – to keep them working. People are the same. They need energy – which they get from food - to keep their bodies working.

(*Hold up the pictures of the foods and drinks.*) What are these? What do we do with food? (We eat it. It goes into our bodies.) What would happen,if you mixed sand or water with the petrol for the car? (The engine would break.) What would happen if the food we put in to our body was dirty or bad? (We would become ill.)

Let's look at a map of our bodies to see where the food we eat goes. (*Pin up an A3 copy of the* ***I can feed myself copymaster****, so that it can easily be seen by all the class.*)

(*Trace the path of the food on the diagram with your finger.*) What does the mouth do? (Chews the food so we can swallow it.) Where does food go next? (Into our stomach.) Draw this tube on yourselves with your finger. Stop when you reach your stomach.

In your stomach special acids break up the food. All the good things in food are used by the body to keep it healthy. These tubes take all the waste things out of your body. Look where waste comes out (the anus). Where do we go to get rid of the waste? (the toilet.)

Follow-up activity

Hand out copies of the **I can feed myself copymaster**. Ask each child to draw some food in the child's hand and then colour in the route the food will take through the body.

Story

The **Nora's cake story** can be used to introduce the concept of the importance of eating a balanced diet.

I can feed myself

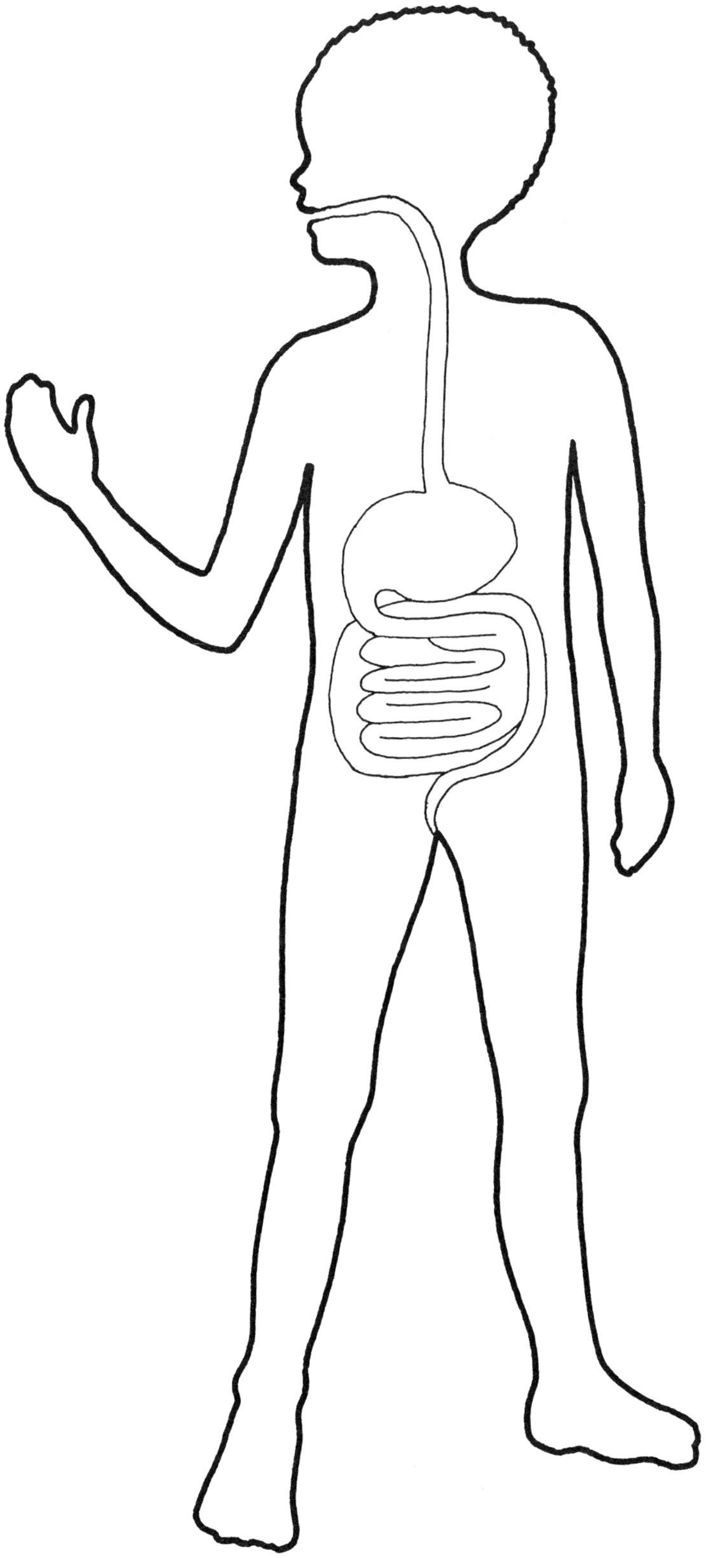

Nora's cake

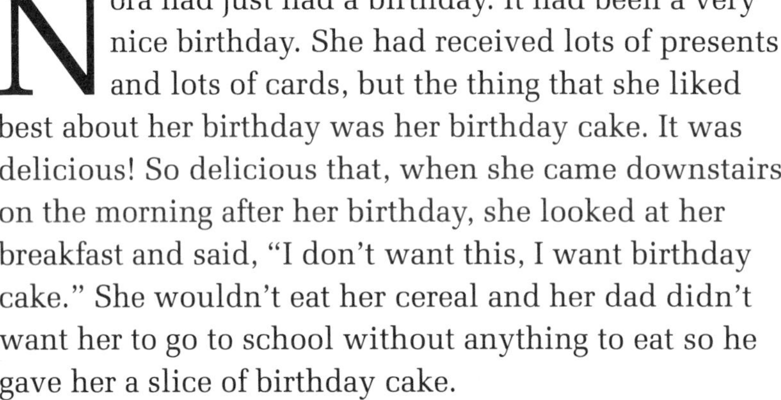

Nora had just had a birthday. It had been a very nice birthday. She had received lots of presents and lots of cards, but the thing that she liked best about her birthday was her birthday cake. It was delicious! So delicious that, when she came downstairs on the morning after her birthday, she looked at her breakfast and said, "I don't want this, I want birthday cake." She wouldn't eat her cereal and her dad didn't want her to go to school without anything to eat so he gave her a slice of birthday cake.

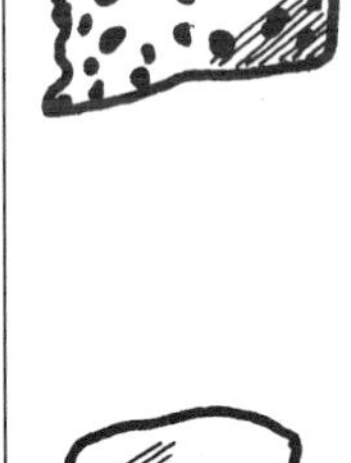

When Nora came home from school her mum asked her, "Did you have a nice day?" But Nora said, "No – I didn't have any lunch." Her mum was very surprised. "Didn't daddy give you your lunch?" she asked. "Yes," said Nora, "but I didn't want it, I wanted birthday cake." "Oh dear," said Mum, "you must be very hungry by now. I'll get your tea." But Nora just pulled a face and said, "I don't want tea, I want birthday cake." And she wouldn't eat anything else.

In fact all that week Nora ate nothing but birthday cake, and by Saturday she had come out in lots of little dark spots so that her dad had to take her to the doctors. "What are these spots?" said Dad to the doctor. The doctor looked very carefully at the spots and said, "I've never seen anything like it. These are not spots, they are currants. I'm afraid your daughter is turning into a birthday cake!"

Dad was very shocked and Nora was very upset. "What can we do?" asked Dad. "She must go to bed and not eat any more birthday cake", said the doctor. And that's exactly what Nora did. She went home straight to bed and after a week she was much better. She never ate birthday cake again – except a very small piece on her birthday because, although birthday cake is very lovely, no one wants to be one!

TIME TO TALK

[Affix school letterhead if required]

Dear Parent/Guardian,

Can you help?
In preparation for a lesson we are having it would be very helpful if you could read this letter from your child.

Eating and drinking

At school we are going to have a lesson about eating and drinking.

Please will you answer these questions for me:

- Do you have a favourite food?
- What is it?
- Why is that your favourite food?
- Do you have a favourite drink?
- What is it?
- Why is that your favourite drink?
- Is there a special meal you can remember?
- Why was it so special?

Thank you for helping me,

6

Happy and sad

HANDLING EMOTIONS

Aim

▶ to help children to understand their emotions and to begin to know how to control them.

Preparation

Before the lesson, send home photocopies of the **Can you help? copymaster** for discussion between the child and parent/guardian.

You will need to use the letters which the children sent to each other in **Lesson 4 – Let me tell you**. [N.B If possible try and make sure that this lesson is held fairly soon after the **Let me tell you** lesson, so that it is still fresh in the childrens' minds.]

Make enough copies of the **Happy and sad copymaster** so that every child can have one each.

Make copies of the **If you're happy and you know it... song**, as necessary.

TIME TO TALK

If you are happy and you know it...

If you're happy and you know it, clap your hands,
If you're happy and you know it, clap your hands,
If you're happy and you know it, and you really want to show it,
If you're happy and you know it, clap your hands

If you're sad and you know it, have a cry,
If you're sad and you know it, have a cry,
If you're sad and you know it, and you really want to show it,
If you're sad and you know it, have a cry

If you're happy and you know it, clap your hands,
If you're happy and you know it, clap your hands,
If you're happy and you know it, and you really want to show it,
If you're happy and you know it, clap your hands

If you're sad and you know it, find a friend,
If you're sad and you know it, find a friend,
If you're sad and you know it, and you really want to show it,
If you're sad and you know it, find a friend

If you're happy and you know it, clap your hands,
If you're happy and you know it, clap your hands,
If you're happy and you know it, and you really want to show it,
If you're happy and you know it, clap your hands

Can you think of any actions to go with this song?

30

Discussion

Points to bring out

- We will all feel happy or sad at some time in our lives.
- We can learn to recognize our feelings.
- We can do things to avoid being sad.
- We can do things to help us feel better when we are sad.

Strategies to try

Choose two children to give out the letters from **Lesson 4 – Let me tell you** (see page 21).

Read and discuss a selection of letters. On a large sheet of paper make a note of some occasions in school which make most children happy and a similar list of occasions which make most children sad.

When something happens to make you happy what does it feel like?
Who likes feeling happy?
Can anyone tell me what it feels like to be sad?
Is it nice to feel sad?
If something makes you sad what do you do? (Cry, talk to someone, have a cuddle, do something you enjoy, find a friend, etc.)

Sad things will happen and there will always be some things that we cannot stop. (If a friend is ill, or moves to another school.) But there are some things that make us feel sad that we can stop. (Arguing, fighting, not sharing, etc.)

Let's have a simple rule to stop sad things like these happening. (For example, if someone is silly or unkind – walk away.)

Make a poster of your special rule.

Follow-up activity

Using the **Happy or sad copymaster** the children choose to make the picture happy or sad. If they decide it is a happy picture they should write something nice in the speech bubble. If they decide it is a sad picture they should write something nasty in the speech bubble.

Song

By carefully choosing appropriate line endings the song can be used as a way of showing the many ways that we can deal with sadness. Further line endings could include: "talk to dad", "talk to mum", "think a nice thought", "have a treat", "watch TV".

Happy and sad

This is a ______________________ picture.

If you are happy and you know it...

If you're happy and you know it, clap your hands,
If you're happy and you know it, clap your hands,
If you're happy and you know it, and you really want to show it,
If you're happy and you know it, clap your hands.

If you're sad and you know it, have a cry,
If you're sad and you know it, have a cry,
If you're sad and you know it, and you really want to show it,
If you're sad and you know it, have a cry.

If you're happy and you know it, clap your hands,
If you're happy and you know it, clap your hands,
If you're happy and you know it, and you really want to show it,
If you're happy and you know it, clap your hands.

If you're sad and you know it, find a friend,
If you're sad and you know it, find a friend,
If you're sad and you know it, and you really want to show it,
If you're sad and you know it, find a friend

If you're happy and you know it, clap your hands,
If you're happy and you know it, clap your hands,
If you're happy and you know it, and you really want to show it,
If you're happy and you know it, clap your hands.

Can you think of any actions to go with this song?

[Affix school letterhead if required]

Dear Parent/Guardian,

Can you help?
In preparation for a lesson we are having it would be very helpful if you could read this letter from your child.

Happy and sad

At school we are having a lesson called "Happy and sad".

- Will you tell me about a time when you were sad?
- Why were you sad?
- Tell me what happened.
- How did you feel?
- Tell me what you did.
- Can you remember a time when you were very happy? Tell me what happened.
- How did you feel?
- Tell me what you did.

Thank you for helping me,

TIMES OF CELEBRATION

7 Invitations

Aims

- to help children to appreciate that special times or events need to be celebrated.
- to emphasise how different cultures celebrate different events.

Preparation

Before the lesson, send home photocopies of the **Can you help? copymaster** for discussion between the child and parent/guardian.

Arrange a time and a venue (hall, classroom, or even outside if fine) when you can organize a small party. If there is an event to celebrate (a feast, festival or special time such as the beginning or end of term) the party could be geared towards it.

Make enough copies of the **Invitations copymaster**, so that every child can have one each.

Have one envelope for every child to put their **Invitations copymasters** in, when they are complete. Set up the Post Box from **Lesson 4 – Let me tell you**.

Make copies of the **Please come poem**, as necessary.

TIME TO TALK

Please come

Would you like to come to my house,
Because I am a king.
I will give you bread and jam to eat,
And a bell for you to ring.

Will you please come to my party,
Where everyone will dance.
And I will sing a song for you,
If you give me the chance.

Would you like to come to tea with me?
We will have cake and squash.
It is our kitten's birthday,
And he likes us to be posh.

Would you like to come to my house,
Because I am a queen.
I will give you nuts and raisins,
And tell you where I've been.

Would you like to come and visit me?
I would like to share with you.
I have so much to celebrate,
And so, I'm sure, have you.

Discussion

Points to bring out

- We all like celebrations.
- Celebrations are a time for sharing.

Strategies to try

Can anyone think of times we celebrate? (Festivals, birthdays, good news, the birth of a new baby, weddings, etc.)

Do we all celebrate the same things?

What ways do we celebrate? (Parties, visits, giving and receiving presents, dressing up, special meals.)

If you were going to have a party who would you invite?

Why would you choose these people? (They are special to us in different ways.)

Does it feel good to celebrate with people who are special to us?

We are all special to each other, so what could we celebrate together as a class?

What will we have at our party? (Food, music, songs, games.) Shall we come in party clothes that day?

Follow-up activity

Put the children into pairs. Each child writes a party invite to their partner, using the **Invitations copymaster**. The children can then post their invites in the class Post Box, and have fun receiving them a few days before the party.

Invitations

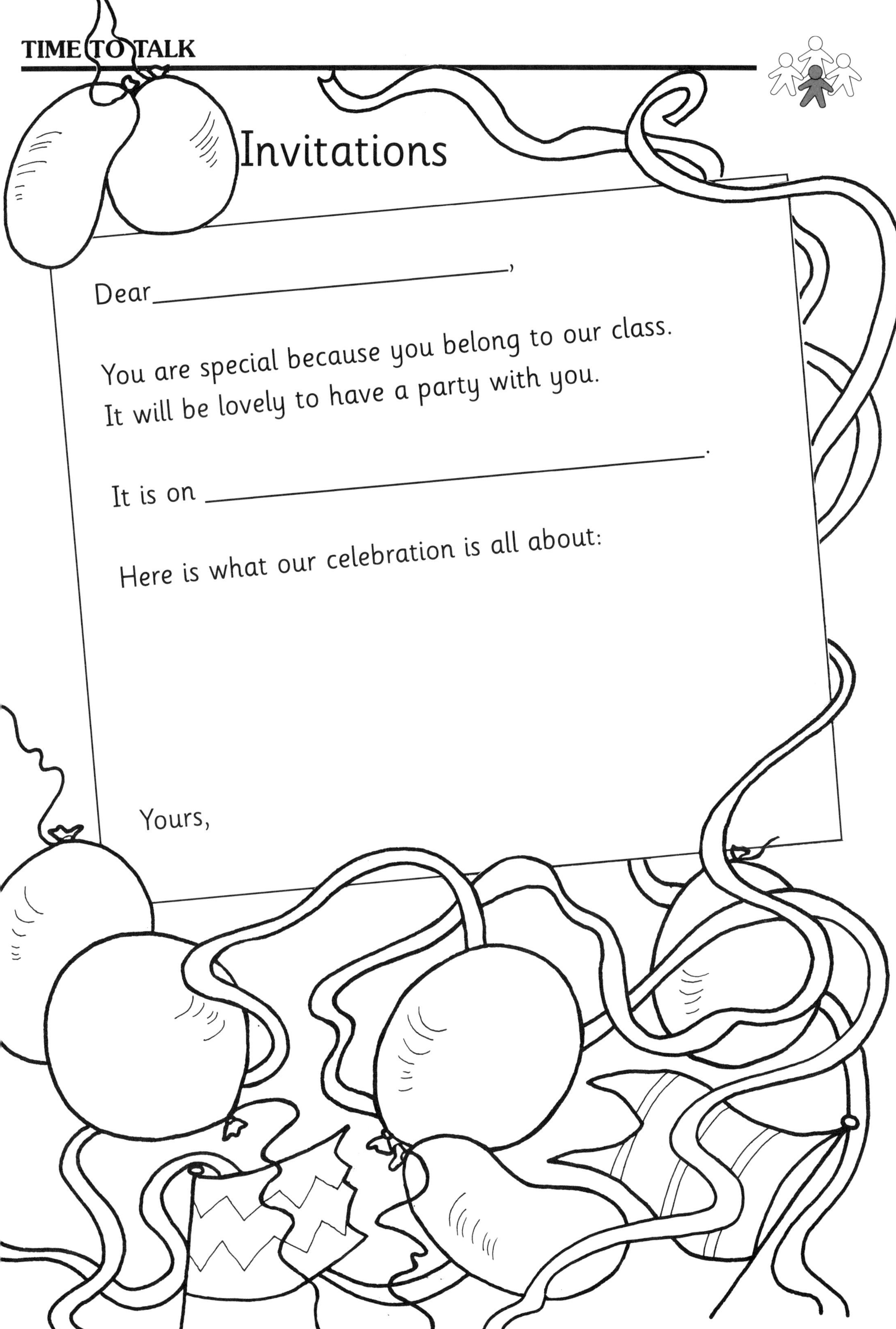

Dear ______________________,

You are special because you belong to our class.
It will be lovely to have a party with you.

It is on ______________________.

Here is what our celebration is all about:

Yours,

Please come

Would you like to come to my house,
Because I am a king.
I will give you bread and jam to eat,
And a bell for you to ring.

Will you please come to my party,
Where everyone will dance.
And I will sing a song for you,
If you give me the chance.

Would you like to come to tea with me?
We will have cake and squash.
It is our kitten's birthday,
And he likes us to be posh.

Would you like to come to my house,
Because I am a queen.
I will give you nuts and raisins,
And tell you where I've been.

Would you like to come and visit me?
I would like to share with you.
I have so much to celebrate,
And so, I'm sure, have you.

[Affix school letterhead if required]

Dear Parent/Guardian,

Can you help?
In preparation for a party we are having on ____________________ it would be very helpful if you could read this letter from your child.

Invitations

Our class is having a celebration at school. We have sent each other invitations. Will you provide something nice: cakes, crisps, biscuits or drinks for our celebration? I will tell you what we are celebrating.

Thank you for helping me,

COMMUNICATION SKILLS

8

Family outings

Aims

- to encourage children to develop their communication skills, by sharing memories of family outings that they have enjoyed.
- to help children to understand that, while some places are fun to visit, there are places where it is dangerous for them to go unaccompanied.

Preparation

Before the lesson, send home photocopies of the **Can you help? copymaster** for discussion between the child and parent/guardian.

Make enough copies of the **Favourite visits maze copymaster** so that the children can all have one each. (Ensure that there is an ample supply of red, green, yellow and black coloured pencils or crayons for the children to use.)

Make copies of the **Places to visit song**, as necessary.

TIME TO TALK

Places to visit

(A singing game sung to the tune of "Here We Go Rond The Mulberry Bush".)

There is a place I like to go, like to go, like to go,
There is a place I like to go,
And the place I like to go is ________

There is a place I shouldn't go, shouldn't go, shouldn't go,
There is a place I shouldn't go,
And the place I shouldn't go is ________

Discussion

Points to bring out

- You don't have to travel a long way from home to have a nice outing – wherever we live there are nice places to visit.
- Different people like different places.
- We like different places for different reasons.
- Some places are not safe to go.

Strategies to try

Who likes to go on outings with their family and friends?

Not all the places we like to go are far away from home. Who knows a place not far away which they like to visit?

Let's sing a song and take it in turns to say where we like to visit and why we like to go there.

The children sing the first verse of the **Places to visit song** and take it in turns/are chosen to talk about a place they like to visit.

All the places we have talked about are places we like to visit. If we are careful they are good places to be.

Sing the second verse of the **Places to visit song** and ask: Does anyone know any places where we shouldn't go? Why?

Follow-up activity

Each child completes the **Favourite visits maze copymaster** by tracing paths, with the correct coloured pencil, to the four 'favourite' places.

Which would be your favourite place to visit? Why?

Favourite visits maze

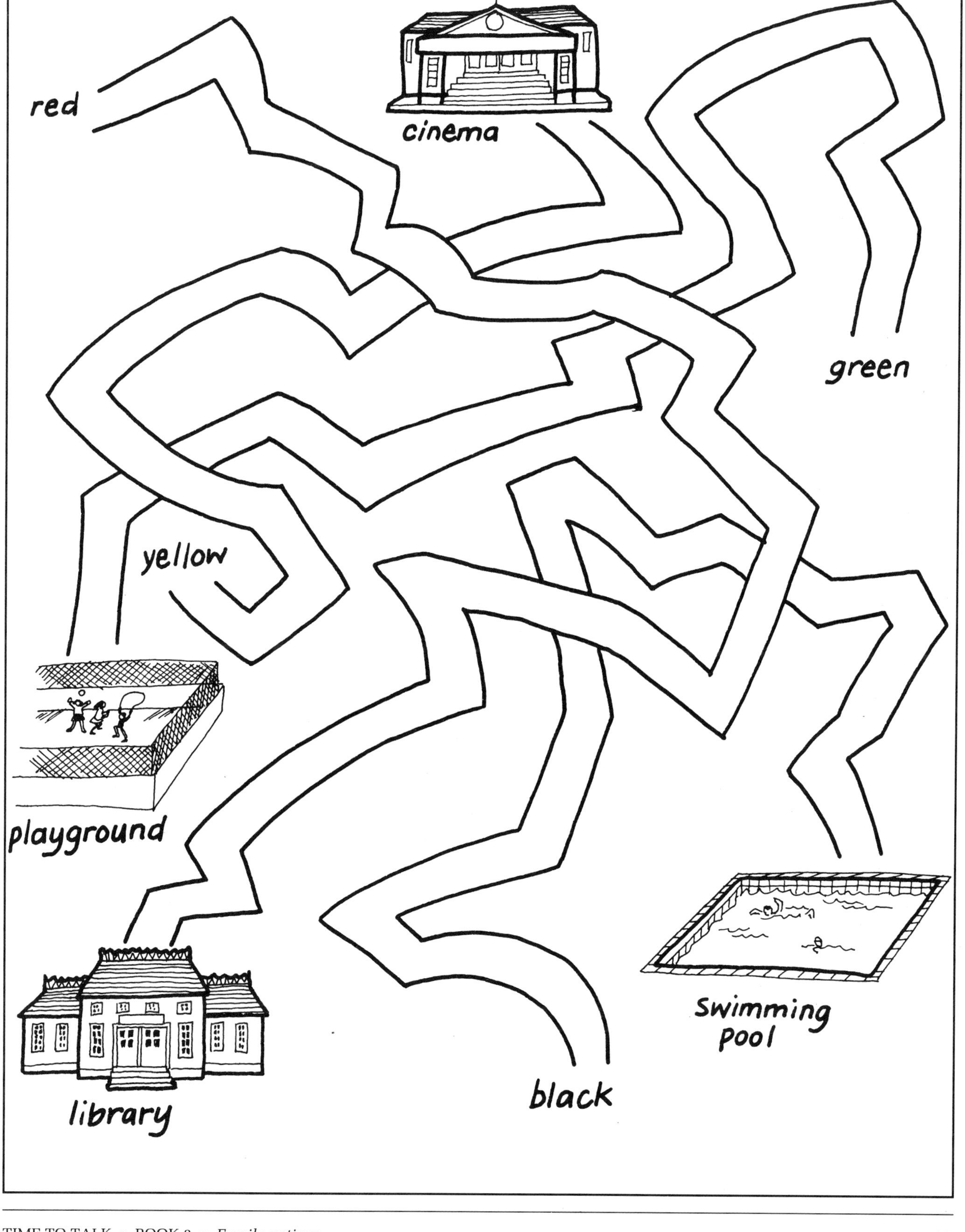

red

cinema

green

yellow

playground

library

black

swimming pool

Places to visit

(A singing game sung to the tune of "Here We Go Rond The Mulberry Bush".)

There is a place I like to go, like to go, like to go,
There is a place I like to go,
And the place I like to go is ___________ .

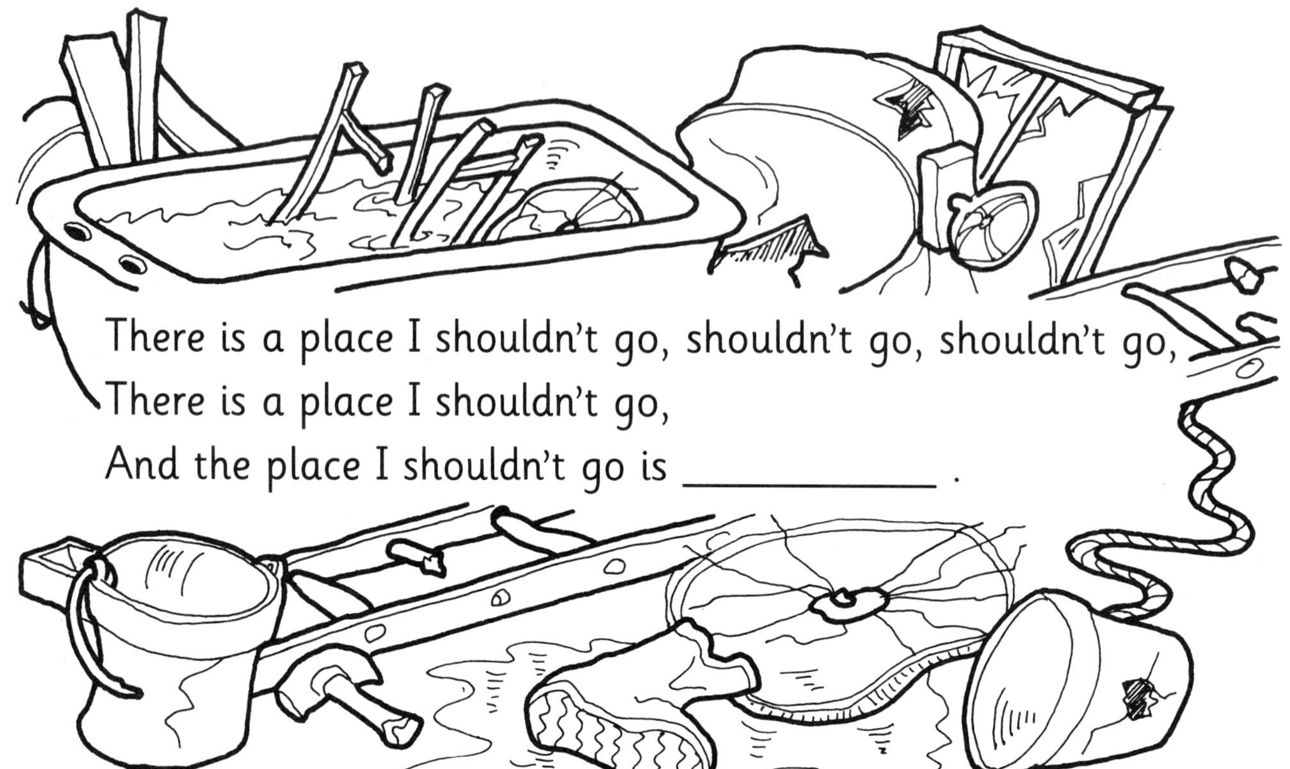

There is a place I shouldn't go, shouldn't go, shouldn't go,
There is a place I shouldn't go,
And the place I shouldn't go is ___________ .

[Affix school letterhead if required]

Dear Parent/Guardian,

Can you help?
In preparation for a lesson we are having it would be very helpful if you could read this letter from your child.

Family outings

At school we are going to have a lesson called "Family outings". I need to think of the place I like to visit best, that is close to home – somewhere like the swimming baths or the cinema. Will you help me to decide what is my favourite place to visit? I also need to think of a place where it isn't safe to go. Can we talk about that as well?

Thank you for helping me,

My family and friends

9 Helping and hurting

PERSONAL RELATIONSHIPS

Aim

- to help children to understand that the way we behave can often affect the way other people feel – if we are helpful we can make people feel happy; if we are hurtful we make people feel sad.

Preparation

Make enough copies of the **I will try copymaster** so that all the children can have one each. (Ensure that suitable materials are available to make the copymasters into either a wall display or a class book.)

Make copies of the **Helping and hurting copymaster**, as necessary. (The children can be given an A4 copy each or an A3 copy – one between two.) Ensure that you have an A3 copy that you can pin to a stiff board and show to the class.

After the lesson, send home copies of the **Can you help? copymaster** for discussion between the child and parent/guardian.

Discussion

Points to bring out

- The way we speak and behave can help or hurt others.
- The way we behave is often influenced by how we feel.

Strategies to try

Look at this poster. (*Show the A3 version of the* ***Helping and hurting copymaster***.)

Let's look at the ways we can help people. (What we say as well as what we do.)

What things that we do can make people happy?

Do we always enjoy doing helpful things? (Cleaning up, going to bed, letting someone else choose what's on TV!)

Why is it good to do helpful things? (Because it shows love and makes people happy.)

What sort of things are hurtful? (Being lazy or selfish.)

Why is it wrong to be hurtful? (It shows a lack of love and it makes people unhappy.)

Are there times when we feel we want to hurt people?

We must all learn to know our feelings. It is normal to sometimes feel angry or to want your own way, but we must not let these feelings hurt others.

Follow-up activity

Ask the children to fill in the **I will try copymasters**, and use them as the basis of a class wall display or to make a class book.

Poster

Hand out copies of the **Helping and hurting copymaster** for the children to colour in and take home. (If it can be arranged, you may want to organize the children into pairs and get them to colour in A3 versions of the copymaster for a class display.)

I will try

I will try to be helpful at school by...

____

____

____

____

____

____

I will try not to be hurtful at school. I won't...

____

____

____

____

____

____

From,

Helping and hurting

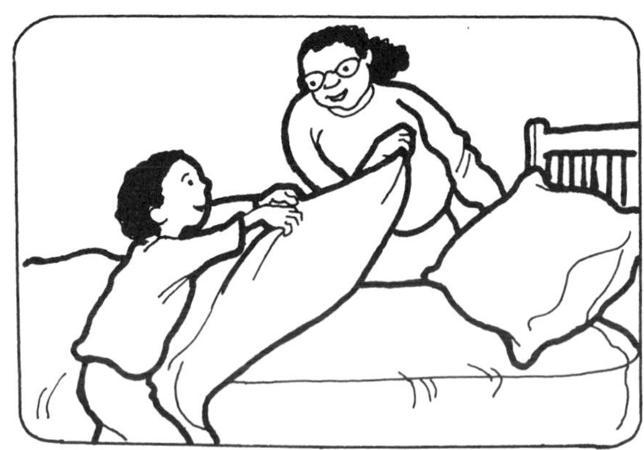

[Affix school letterhead if required]

Dear Parent/Guardian,

Can you help?
As a follow-up to a lesson that we have had, it would be very helpful if you could read this letter from your child.

I promise. I promise. I promise. I promise. I promise. I promise. I promise. I promise. I promise.

Helping and hurting

Will you help me to choose two things to try and do to be more helpful at home? Will you help me write them down?
I will be more helpful by...

____

____

Will you tell me about the hurtful things that I sometimes do, and help me try not to be hurtful at home?
I won't...

____

____

Please will you put this sheet up somewhere that I can look at it, to remind me what I have promised?

Thank you for helping me,

CARE IN ILLNESS

10

When I am ill

Aims

- to help children develop an awareness of the nature of health care within the community.
- to lead them on to understand the importance of caring for the sick.

Preparation

Before the lesson send home photocopies of the **Can you help? copymaster** for discussion between the child and parent/guardian.

Invite someone who has been ill in hospital to talk to the children. (If appropriate, you may want to do this yourself, or ask a colleague to come and talk to the class.) Ask them to tell the story of how they became ill, how they felt about how they were looked after, and how they got better.

Make enough copies of the **Thank you... copymaster** so that all the children can have a copy each.

Make copies of **Wilfred's story**, as necessary

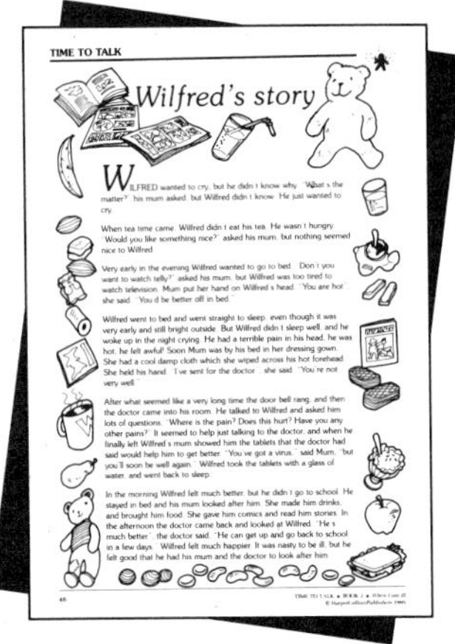
TIME TO TALK

Wilfred's story

WILFRED wanted to cry, but he didn't know why. "What's the matter?" his mum asked, but Wilfred didn't know. He just wanted to cry.

When tea time came, Wilfred didn't eat his tea. He wasn't hungry. "Would you like something nice?" asked his mum, but nothing seemed nice to Wilfred.

Very early in the evening Wilfred wanted to go to bed. "Don't you want to watch telly?" asked his mum, but Wilfred was too tired to watch television. Mum put her hand on Wilfred's head. "You are hot", she said. "You'd be better off in bed."

Wilfred went to bed and went straight to sleep, even though it was very early and still bright outside. But Wilfred didn't sleep well, and he woke up in the night crying. He had a terrible pain in his head, he was hot, he felt awful! Soon Mum was by his bed in her dressing gown. She had a cool damp cloth which she wiped across his hot forehead. She held his hand. "I've sent for the doctor", she said. "You're not very well."

After what seemed like a very long time the door bell rang, and then the doctor came into his room. He talked to Wilfred and asked him lots of questions. "Where is the pain? Does this hurt? Have you any other pains?" It seemed to help just talking to the doctor, and when he finally left Wilfred's mum showed him the tablets that the doctor had said would help him to get better. "You've got a virus," said Mum, "but you'll soon be well again." Wilfred took the tablets with a glass of water, and went back to sleep.

In the morning Wilfred felt much better, but he didn't go to school. He stayed in bed and his mum looked after him. She made him drinks, and brought him food. She gave him comics and read him stories. In the afternoon the doctor came back and looked at Wilfred. "He's much better", the doctor said. "He can get up and go back to school in a few days." Wilfred felt much happier. It was nasty to be ill, but he felt good that he had his mum and the doctor to look after him.

Discussion

Points to bring out:

- We should care for people who are ill.
- Often members of our family look after us when we are ill.
- There are people whose job it is to look after the sick.

Strategies to try

Ask the visitor to talk about when and why they were in hospital. After the talk, ask the visitor one or two questions:

Do you have to be very ill to go to hospital?

Why is hospital special?

Then ask the children:

If you were ill, but not in hospital, who would look after you? Can any of you remember being ill? What was it like?

How many people can you name that look after us when we are ill?

What about when our eyes don't work properly?

Has anyone ever had to go and see a 'specialist'

The discussion may also give you the opportunity to talk about delicate subjects such as mental health.

Follow-up activity

Ask the children to colour in the **Thank you...copymaster** and draw a picture/write about a time when they were ill. The copymaster can then be given to the person that the child wants to thank, e.g. a parent, a grandparent, a health visitor, the school nurse, etc. (The children needent have been *very* ill – they could thank someone for looking after them after a fall in the playground, or when they had a stomach upset or toothache.)

Story

Wilfred's story can be told, either as an introduction to the discussion or as a close to the day.

Thank you for looking after me when I was not very well

Wilfred's story

WILFRED wanted to cry, but he didn't know why. "What's the matter?" his mum asked, but Wilfred didn't know. He just wanted to cry.

When tea time came, Wilfred didn't eat his tea. He wasn't hungry. "Would you like something nice?" asked his mum, but nothing seemed nice to Wilfred.

Very early in the evening Wilfred wanted to go to bed. "Don't you want to watch telly?" asked his mum, but Wilfred was too tired to watch television. Mum put her hand on Wilfred's head. "You are hot", she said. "You'd be better off in bed."

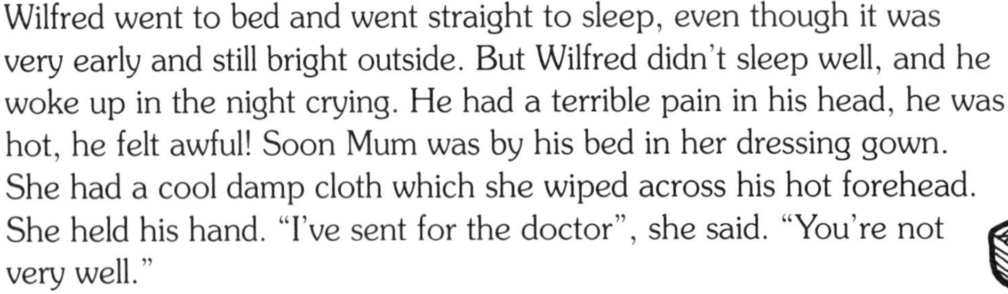

Wilfred went to bed and went straight to sleep, even though it was very early and still bright outside. But Wilfred didn't sleep well, and he woke up in the night crying. He had a terrible pain in his head, he was hot, he felt awful! Soon Mum was by his bed in her dressing gown. She had a cool damp cloth which she wiped across his hot forehead. She held his hand. "I've sent for the doctor", she said. "You're not very well."

After what seemed like a very long time the door bell rang, and then the doctor came into his room. He talked to Wilfred and asked him lots of questions. "Where is the pain? Does this hurt? Have you any other pains?" It seemed to help just talking to the doctor, and when he finally left Wilfred's mum showed him the tablets that the doctor had said would help him to get better. "You've got a virus," said Mum, "but you'll soon be well again." Wilfred took the tablets with a glass of water, and went back to sleep.

In the morning Wilfred felt much better, but he didn't go to school. He stayed in bed and his mum looked after him. She made him drinks, and brought him food. She gave him comics and read him stories. In the afternoon the doctor came back and looked at Wilfred. "He's much better", the doctor said. "He can get up and go back to school in a few days." Wilfred felt much happier. It was nasty to be ill, but he felt good that he had his mum and the doctor to look after him.

[Affix school letterhead if required]

Dear Parent/Guardian,

Can you help?
In preparation for a lesson we are having it would be very helpful if you could read this letter from your child.

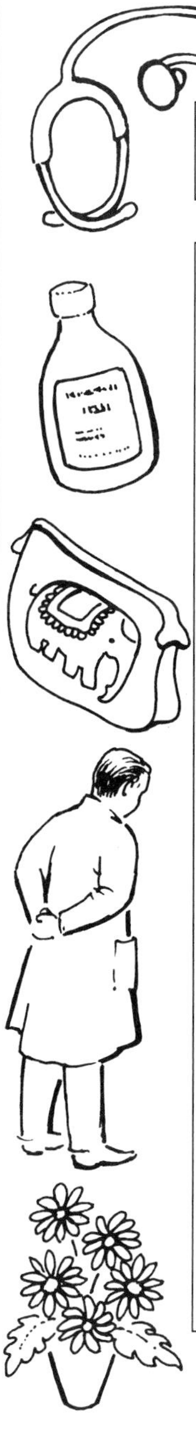

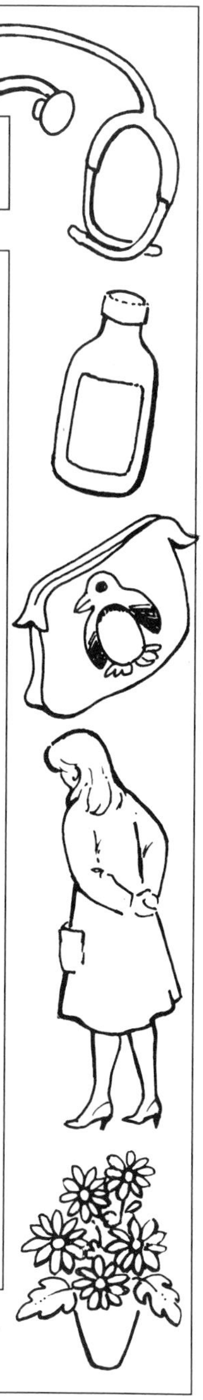

When I am ill

At school we are going to have a lesson called "When I am ill". We will be talking about being looked after in hospital.

Could you tell me:

- Have you ever looked after me when I was ill?
- What was the matter with me?
- What did you do?
- Have I ever been in hospital?
- What was the matter with me?
- Do you think doctors and nurses do their jobs well?

Thank you for helping me,

My family and friends

11 Good and bad

MAKING JUDGEMENTS

Aims

- to explain to children why, in our everyday lives, we are attracted to good and bad things.
- to help children learn how, by understanding our emotions, we can learn to control them.

Preparation

Before the lesson, send home photocopies of the **Can you help? copymaster** for discussion between the child and parent/guardian.

Enlarge a copy of the **Good and bad song** to show and sing with the children at the start of the lesson. Make copies for the children, as necessary. (Make sure the children have their completed **Can you help? copymaster** to hand.)

Pin up two large sheets of paper (for the 'good' and 'bad' lists).

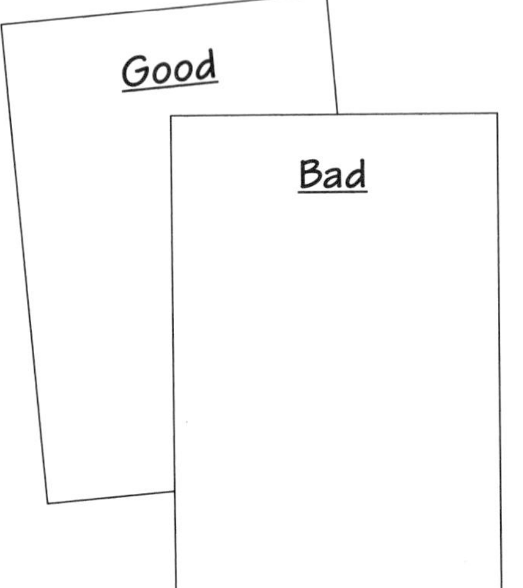

Make enough copies of the **Making choices copymaster** so that all the children can have one each. (Ensure that red and blue pencils/crayons are available for the children to use.)

Discussion

Points to bring out

- Good things help and support people.
- Bad things make people unhappy.

Strategies to try

Here is a song (**The good and bad song**). Let's us sing the song and make two lists; one list of things that are good and one list of things that are bad. (The children can refer to their **Can you help? copymasters** for ideas.)

When the song is finished ask the following questions:

Let's look at the list.
What can we say about good things? (They help and support people.)
What can we say about bad things? (They make people unhappy.)
What other things from school and home can we add to the list?
Sometimes we like to do good things. Why?
Sometimes we like to do bad things. Why? (*This may be a difficult discussion, and will need carefull handling.*)
We can all choose the way we want to behave, but we need each other's help to choose to be good.

Follow-up activity

Ask the children to colour in the **Making choices copymaster**, following the instructions carefully.

Making choices

Colour the things that are good in blue.
Colour the things that bad in red.

Telling lies

Telling the truth

Stealing

Bullying

Sharing

Being a good friend

The good and bad song

(A song sung to the tune of "Nick Nack Paddywack".)

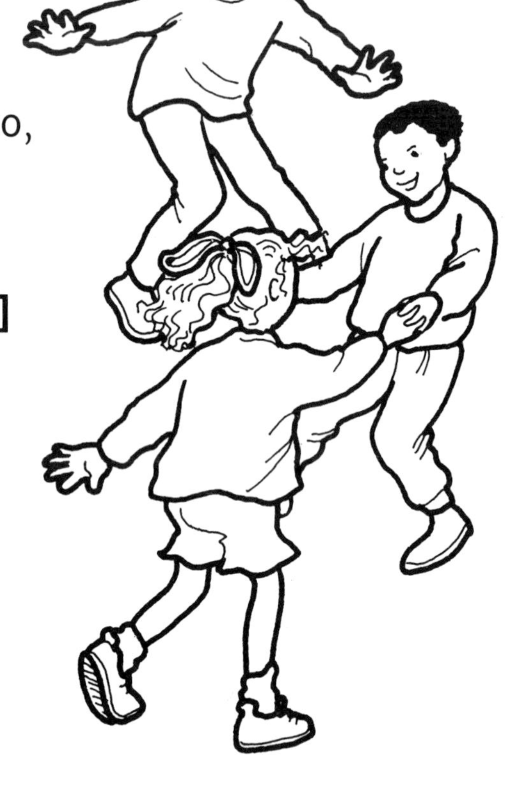

Good and bad – good and bad,
Good is happy and bad is sad.
Playing with my friends is good to do,
Can you think of a good thing too?

[Take a suggestion from a child.]

Good and bad – good and bad,
Good is happy and bad is sad.
Fighting on the playground is bad to do,
Can you think of a bad thing too?

[Take a suggestion from a child.]

[Affix school letterhead if required]

Dear Parent/Guardian,

Can you help?
In preparation for a lesson we are having it would be very helpful if you could read this letter from your child.

GOOD BAD GOOD BAD GOOD

Good and bad

At school we are going to have a lesson called "Good and bad". Will you sit with me for a while and help me to write a list of things that are bad (like stealing) and things that are good (like telling the truth).
It is good to...

____

____

____

It is bad to...

____

____

____

Will you remind me to put this list in my school bag so that I can look at it again when we have our lesson?

Thank you for helping me,

GOOD BAD GOOD BAD GOOD

ORGANIZATIONAL SKILLS

12 Come and visit

Aims

- to encourage children to consider the work involved organizing events.
- to help the children to organize a visit to the school for their parents/guardians.

Preparation

Arrange a free period in the school hall or (if it is warm and dry) playground when families can be invited to visit. Select from the *Time to Talk* series, or from other sources, some well known and liked games and songs. Arrange to have light refreshments available.

Have a large sheet of paper ready for the 'If we were to organize a visit, what things would we have to think about?' list.

After the lesson, send home photocopies of the **Can you help? copymaster** (filling in all relevant details) and the **Will you come? copymasters**.

Make copies of the **We like to... song**, as necessary.

TIME TO TALK

The we like to... song

(A clapping song sung to the tune of "Here We Go Round The Mulberry Bush".)

At the end of each verse who will be the first to put up their hand and suggest what we need?

We like to sing, and we like to play,
We like to play, we like to play
We like to sing, and we like to play
What do we need go on holiday?

Can you name something that we need to go on holiday?

We like to sing, and we like to play,
We like to play, we like to play
We like to sing, and we like to play
What do we need to go on an outing all day?

Can you name something that we need to go on an outing?

We like to sing, and we like to play,
We like to play, we like to play
We like to sing, and we like to play
What do we need to go swimming?

Can you name something that we need to go swimming?

Discussion

Points to bring out

- Even things we do every day need some organizing.
- Usually Mum and Dad organize things for us.
- It is a kind and thoughtful thing to organize a visit.

Strategies to try

Think about the things that Mum and Dad do every day – take us to school, make us a packed lunch, etc.

Think about the special things that we sometimes do – visit relatives, go swimming, go on holiday.

All these things, the things that we do every day, and the special things, need to be carefully organized.

What things have to be organized to make sure we get to school? (Getting up at the right time, making sure there are clean clothes to wear and food for breakfast, etc.)

What sort of things would we have to think about if we arranged a holiday? (Where to go, when, how to get there, etc.)

Who would like to help organize a visit for the mums and dads? (You may want to include brothers/sisters/grandparents.)

Pin up the large sheet of paper and ask: "If we were to organize a visit, what things would we have to think about?" Try and include: When/where would people come? (If outdoors, what if it rained?) Who would we invite? How would we let them know about the visit? Would we play games and sing songs? Which games and songs should we choose? Would there be food/drink – who would provide it?

Follow-up activity

Hand out copies of the **Will you come? copymaster**. The children draw/write an invitation for their parents and take it home, along with the **Can you help? copymaster** (which should contain all relevant details of the visit to avoid possible confusion).

Song
The children can learn the **We like to... song** and show it to the parents when they come to visit.

Will you come?

The we like to... song

(A clapping song sung to the tune of "Here We Go Round The Mulberry Bush".)

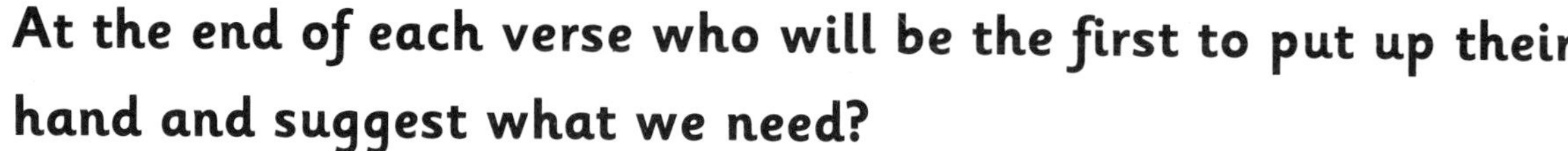

At the end of each verse who will be the first to put up their hand and suggest what we need?

We like to sing, and we like to play,
We like to play, we like to play.
We like to sing, and we like to play
What do we need go on holiday?

Can you name something that we need to go on holiday?

We like to sing, and we like to play,
We like to play, we like to play.
We like to sing, and we like to play
What do we need to go on an outing all day?

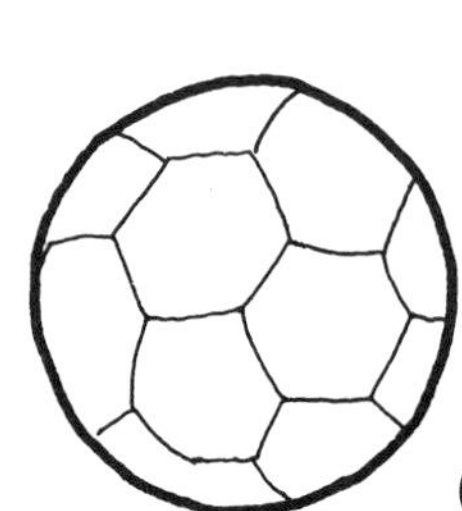

Can you name something that we need to go on an outing?

We like to sing, and we like to play,
We like to play, we like to play.
We like to sing, and we like to play
What do we need to go swimming?

Can you name something that we need to go swimming?

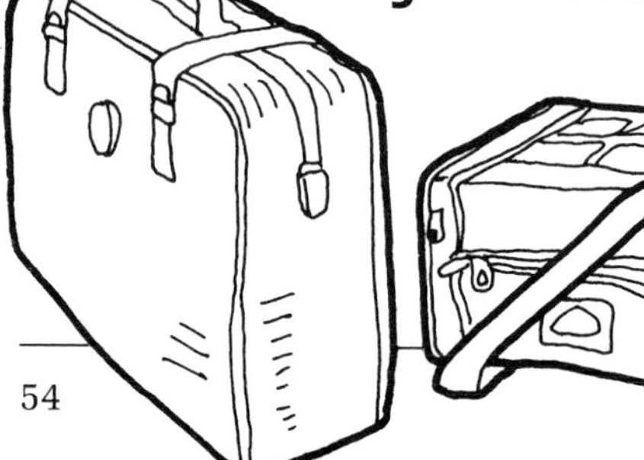

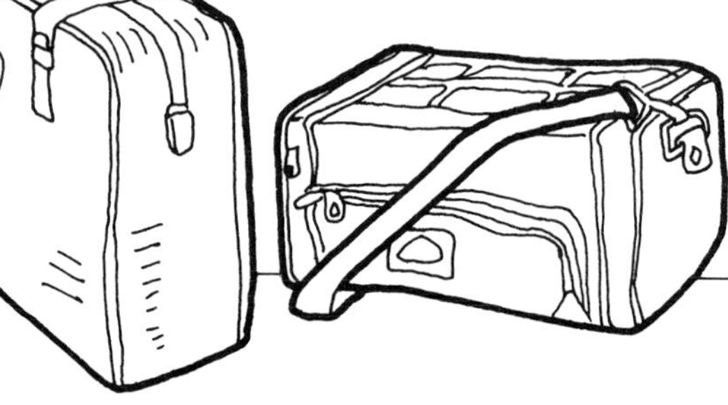

[Affix school letterhead if required]

Dear Parent/Guardian,

As part of a lesson called "Come and visit" our children are organizing a visit in school for parents and guardians.

The visit will take place on ______________________________.

and will be held ________________________________.

Food and drinks will be available, and the children have arranged games and songs to show you.

It would be helpful if we could anticipate numbers. Please could you fill in this reply slip and give it to your child to bring back to school.

I will/will not be coming to visit the school on _______________.

There will be _____ of us visiting.

[Please insert name here:] ______________________________.

Thank you,

13 The clinic

LOCAL HEALTH CARE ENVIRONMENT

Aim

- to help children to learn about the health services that are available to them at their local clinic.

Preparation

Before the lesson, send home photocopies of the **Can you help? copymaster** for discussion between the child and parent/guardian.

Invite a mum into school to talk to the children about taking a baby to the clinic. Ask her to talk about why we need clinics, what happens there, the sort of people she meets, how she travels to the clinic, how many people use the clinic, etc.

Find out what further services the local clinic offers.

Collect any attractive or informative posters that the clinic may have available.

Make enough copies of the **A visit to the clinic copymaster** so that the children can all have one each.

Make copies of the **Who uses the clinic? copymaster** – one A3 copy which can be put on display, and A4 copies for the children to colour and put in their files.

Discussion

Points to bring out

- Clinics are important places.
- The local clinic offers services to local people to help them to keep healthy.
- The clinic serves lots of people of different ages.

Strategies to try

When a mum has a baby she likes to make sure the baby is properly cared for. Today _______________ is going to tell us about how the clinic helps/helped her to care for her baby.

Invite the mum to talk about the clinic. Encourage the children to ask questions during or after the talk, whichever is more helpful to the speaker. At the end of the talk follow up with some questions for the children:

How many of you have been to the clinic? Why did you go?

Show the enlarged copy of the **Who uses the clinic? copymaster** and ask the children to think about the question. Talk about other services the clinic offers and explain what they are and who they serve. (*Use any posters/leaflets you may have collected to illustrate these services.*)

Follow-up activity

The children colour in the **A visit to the clinic copymaster** and write about the clinic, or a time that they visited the clinic in the space provided.

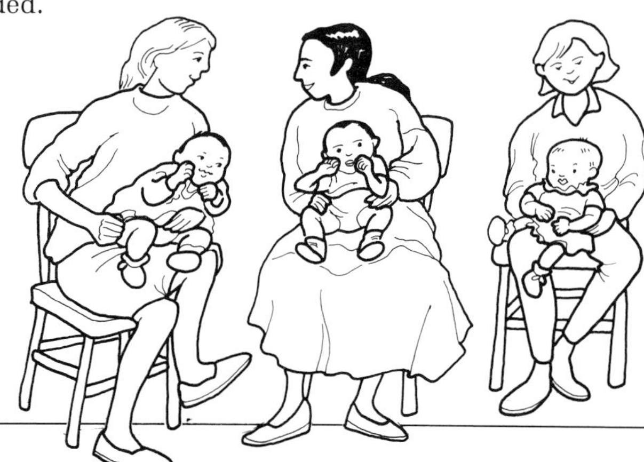

A visit to the clinic

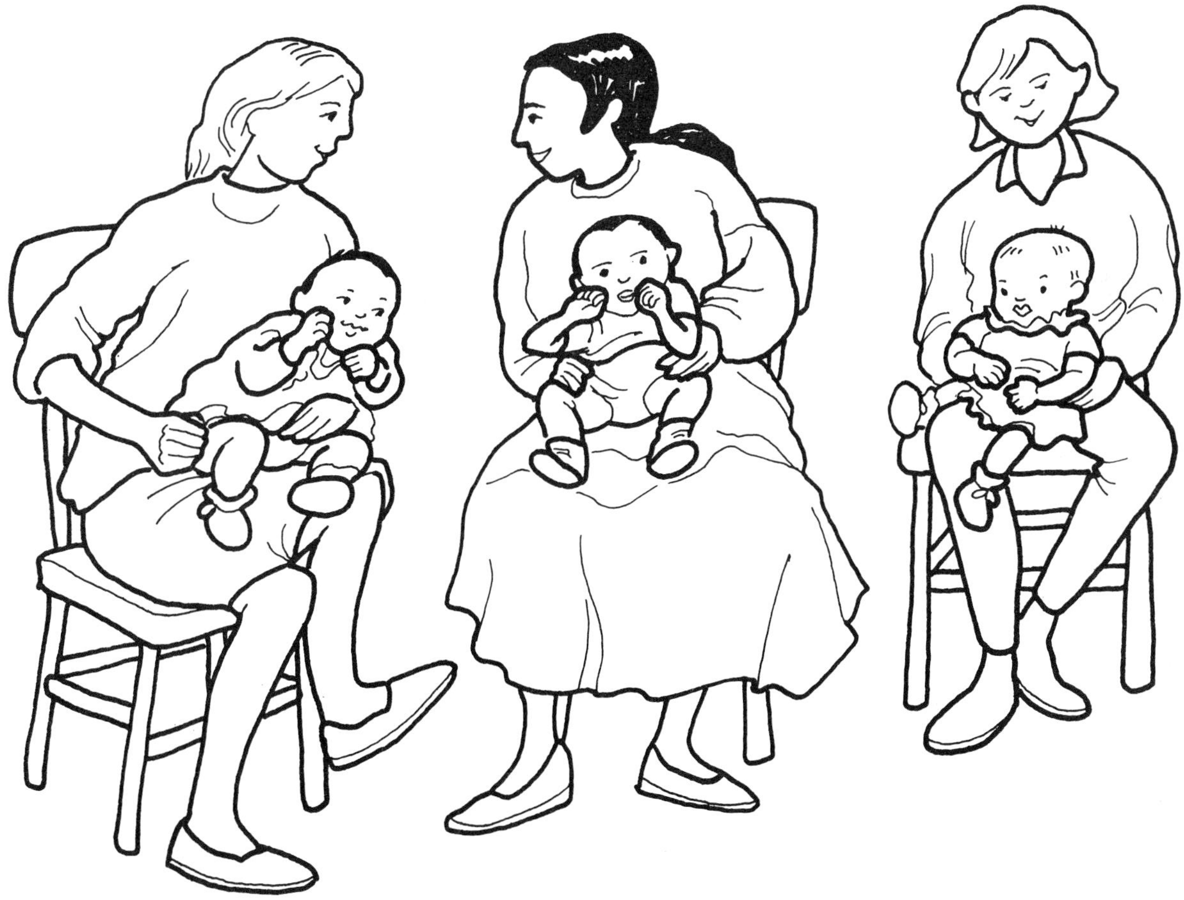

Who uses the clinic?

WE ALL USE OUR CLINIC.

[Affix school letterhead if required]

Dear Parent/Guardian,

Can you help?
In preparation for a lesson we are having it would be very helpful if you could read this letter from your child.

The clinic

At school we are having a lesson called "The clinic".

Can you tell me about the clinic in our local area?

- Did you take me to the clinic when I was a baby?
- What sort of services does the clinic offer?
- Do you still go to the clinic?
- Why?

Thank you for helping me,

14 My school

THE SCHOOL ENVIRONMENT

Aims

- to help children to appreciate that we share our school with others, and must move through it carefully without disturbing people.
- to lead the children on to think about how they should behave in places, outside of school, that they share with others.

Preparation

Before the lesson, send home photocopies of the **Can you help? copymaster** for discussion between the child and parent/guardian.

Take ten (vary this number as you see fit) photographs of different places inside and outside the school which are accessible to the children in your class. Also take three photographs of places in school that are out of bounds to the children. (The places you choose should be a mixture of areas well known, and little known, to the children.) Have ten 'rewards' or 'treasures' (sweets or sticky badges) to hand out to the children at the end of the activity.

Make enough copies of the **My favourite place in school copymaster** so that all of the children can have a copy each.

Make copies of the **My school song**, as necessary.

TIME TO TALK

My school song

(A song sung to the tune of "Ba Ba Black Sheep")

At our school we work and play,
Learn a new thing every day
Reading, writing numbers too
Learning things is good for you

At our school we meet our friends,
Help each other 'till the school day ends
Playing catch,
Or playing chase
Our school is such a lovely place

At our school we learn to grow,
Learn the things we need to know
I am me,
And you are you
We hope that you love our school too!

Can you do the actions to this song?

Discussion

Points to bring out

- There are lots of different places in and around our school.
- We are not allowed in some places and not in others.
- There are good reasons why we are allowed in some places and not allowed in others.

Strategies to try

I have some photographs for you to look at. (*Hold up a photo of a well known place.*)

Where is this? (*Don't let the children call out answers until everyone has seen it.*)

Continue, putting the photos into two piles – places that are easy for the children to identify, and places that are more difficult.

Our school has lots of different places in it. Some of the places shown in these photos are places that you are not allowed in. (*Give examples and reasons.*)

Choose photos of places that are accessible to the children. Give each group one photo.

I want each group to decide where in the school they would go to find the place in their picture. (*Take one suggestion from each group.*)

Before you go and look for the place in the picture let's make three rules for moving through the school: 1. We never run; 2. We make no noise; 3. We don't disturb anyone. (You may want to change or adapt these rules.)

Now go and find the places in the photos. (Groups may need to be accompanied by an adult or an older child)

When the children return 'treasure' is given to those who located the place shown in their photo. The activity can be repeated until all the photos are identified.

Follow-up activity

The children complete the **My favourite place in school copymaster** in whichever way is appropriate to their ability.

My favourite place in school is:

My school song

(A song sung to the tune of "Ba Ba Black Sheep".)

At our school we work and play,
Learn a new thing every day.
Reading, writing numbers too.
Learning things is good for you.

At our school we meet our friends,
Help each other 'till the school day ends.
Playing catch,
Or playing chase.
Our school is such a lovely place.

At our school we learn to grow,
Learn the things we need to know.
I am me,
And you are you.
We hope that you love our school too!

Can you do the actions to this song?

[Affix school letterhead if required]

Dear Parent/Guardian,

Can you help?
In preparation for a lesson we are having it would be very helpful if you could you read this letter from your child.

My school

In school we are going to have a lesson about places we are allowed to go and places we are not allowed to go in our school.

Can you tell me:

- Are there any places where I am not allowed to go near home?
- Why? (Is it because it isn't safe, or because it is private?)
- How many people do I share home with?
- Why is it important that I think about the other people I share home with?

Thank you for helping me,

15

Places I like to visit

THE WIDER ENVIRONMENT

Aims

- to encourage children to think about places, away from home, that they have visited.
- to lead children on to an awareness of the wider environment that exists outside of their own community.

Preparation

Before the lesson, send home photocopies of the **Can you help? copymaster** for discussion between the child and parent/guardian.

Make enough copies of the **Wish you were here copymaster** so that all the children can have one each.

Make copies of **The places game**, as necessary. (You will need 3 large hoops to play this game.)

Ensure that you have a supply of photo hinges (or some other method of securing photos in place without damaging them).

TIME TO TALK

The places game

(A singing game.)

Monday, Monday, Monday,
Can we go out today?
Monday, Monday, Monday,
Where can we go and play?

Tuesday, Tuesday, Tuesday,
Can we go out today?
Tuesday, Tuesday, Tuesday,
Where can we go and play?

Wednesday, Wednesday, Wednesday,
Can we go out to today?
Wednesday, Wednesday, Wednesday,
Where can we go and play?

Can you name the rest of the days of the week? Write them down.

Discussion

Points to bring out

- We have all been away from home at some time.
- There are lots of different places that we can visit.
- Often, the places that we visit are very different from the places we live in.

Strategies to try

Ask the children who have brought photographs in to take it in turns to talk about them.

Do you remember this outing/holiday?

Where did you go? (*Encourage the children to talk about the place that they visited.*)

Do you know how far away from home you travelled?

Did you visit a different town/county/country?

What was it like? Was it the same as home or very different?

Were the people the same as the people you know at home or were they very different? (If yes, in what way were they different, e.g they spoke a different language.)

Follow-up activity

Hand out the **Wish you were here copymasters**. Give photo hinges to those children who have brought in photographs, and show them how to use them to stick their photos onto the blank space on the copymaster. (Those children who haven't brought in photos can draw their own 'postcard'). Ask the children to write in the space provided who the card is 'to', and to write a short message about their holiday.

Game

Place 3 hoops on the floor. Decide before hand which places each of the hoops represents (e.g. the seaside, a funfair, the park).

The children stand in a circle around the hoops and sing the first verse from **The places game**, while one child (chosen before the game started) skips around the inside of the circle. When the song stops that child chooses one of the hoops and stands in it. The game continues until all of the children are standing in a hoop.

Wish you were here

The places game

(A singing game.)

Monday, Monday, Monday,
Can we go out today?
Monday, Monday, Monday,
Where can we go and play?

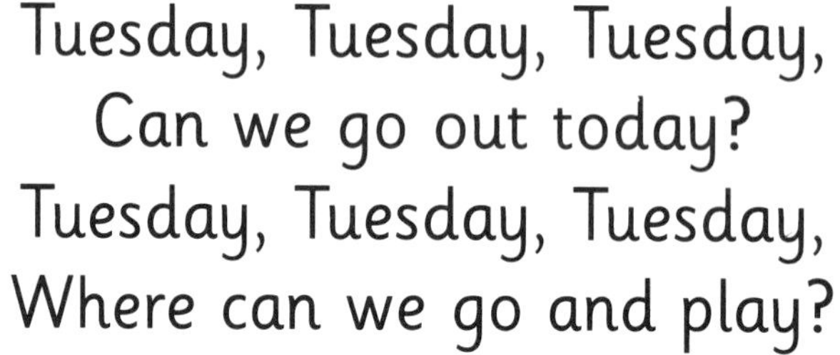

Tuesday, Tuesday, Tuesday,
Can we go out today?
Tuesday, Tuesday, Tuesday,
Where can we go and play?

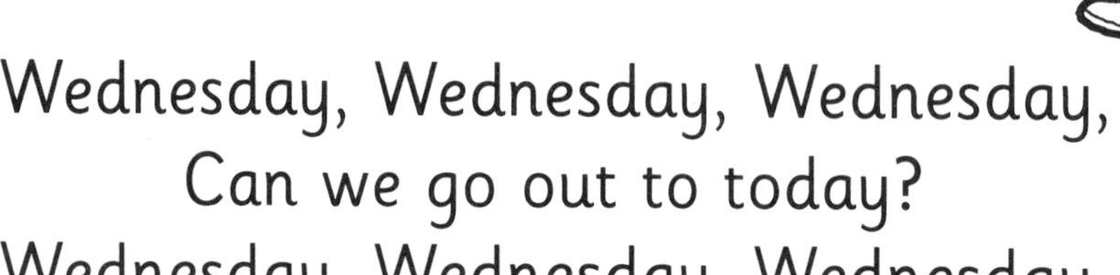

Wednesday, Wednesday, Wednesday,
Can we go out to today?
Wednesday, Wednesday, Wednesday,
Where can we go and play?

**Can you name the rest of the days of the week?
Write them down.**

[Affix school letterhead if required]

Dear Parent/Guardian,

Can you help?
In preparation for a lesson we are having it would be very helpful if you could read this letter from your child.

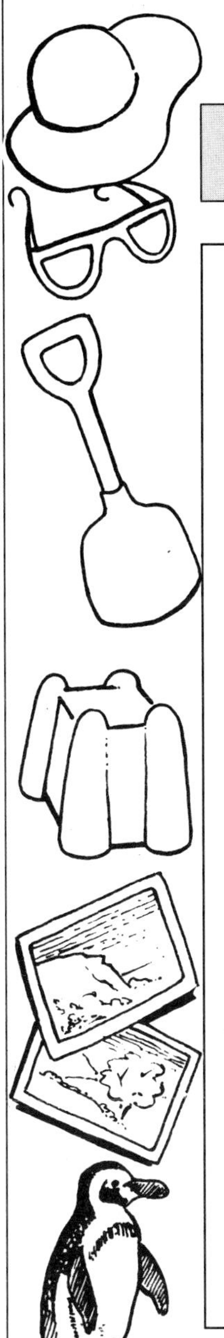

Places I like to visit

In school we are having a lesson called "Places I like to visit".

Please could you help me to choose a photograph of an outing or holiday that I have been on, and put it in an envelope for me to take to school.
I will bring it back safely when I have finished with it.

If we don't have any photographs, please could you tell me about a holiday or outing we have been on.

- Where did we go?
- When did we go there?
- Did we have a good time? Can you remind me of some of the nice things that we did?

Thank you for helping me,

16 People I see

PEOPLE IN THE COMMUNITY

Aim

- to help children to understand how their community is made up of many different people.

Preparation

Before the lesson, hand out photocopies of the **Can you help? copymaster**. Ask the children to choose someone to give it to. (Either a relative, a friend from school or a member of the school staff.)

Collect six pictures of very different people from whatever sources are available (magazines, newspapers, etc).

Make enough copies of the **People I see copymaster** so that all the children can have one each. (Make sure that every child has a blank sheet of paper to write their ideas on.)

Make copies of the **Look at me song**, as necessary.

Discussion

Points to bring out

- There are lots of different people in our community.
- We do not know most of the people in our community.
- As we get older we begin to know more people.

Strategies to try

Here are some pictures of lots of different people. Let's pretend we know these people. Let's pretend they live near us.

(*Hold up a picture.*) Who could this be? Let's invent a name for this person.

Where might we see him/her? Could it be someone who works somewhere like a shop? Let's decide what this person does. (*Repeat this for each picture.*)

Can you think of anyone who you see often but whose name you do not know?

Think of all the people that we see regularly but we do not know (e.g. the crossing attendant).

Follow-up activity

Ask the children to colour in the **People I see copymaster**, and to write on a separate piece of paper what they know about the people in the pictures.

Game

The children sit in a circle. One child is chosen to stand in the circle and mime a job. The children all sing the verse from the **Look at me copymaster**. When the song is finished, the first child to put up their hand and guess correctly what the mime was stands up in the centre of the circle and does a mime of their own.

People I see

Write what you can about these people.

Look at me

(A singing game sung to the tune of "This Old Man".)

Look at me.

Look at me.

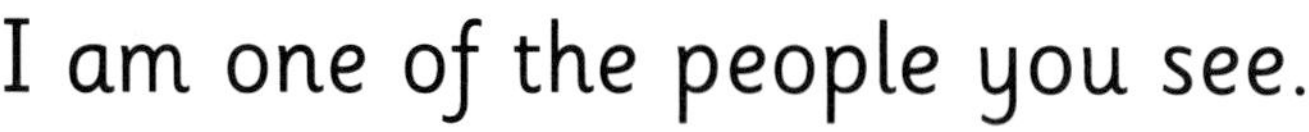

I am one of the people you see.

I am roundabout every day.

Who am I?

Oh can you say?

[Affix school letterhead if required]

Dear Friend,

Can you help?
In preparation for a lesson we are having it would be very helpful if you read this letter from one of our children.

People I see

In school we are having a lesson about all the different sorts of people who live in our community.

Please will you tell me a little bit about yourself? Will you tell me:

- Where were you born?
- Where do you live?
- Do you have a job? What do you do?

Can you tell me one thing about yourself that makes you special?

Thank you for helping me,

17
Busy places

SERVICES IN THE COMMUNITY

Aim

- ▶ to encourage children to become aware of the nature and function of different services within our community.

Preparation

Before the lesson, send home photocopies of the **Can you help? copymaster** for discussion between the child and parent/guardian.

Collect a selection of items from 'busy places' (e.g. a supermarket, a burger-bar, a cinema, a bowling rink, etc.) in the locality.

Cut out a selection of pictures of factories, offices and holiday resorts (other busy places) from old magazines.

Make enough photocopies of **The busy place copymaster** so that all the children can have a copy each.

Make copies of the **Where am I? game**, as necessary.

TIME TO TALK

Where am I?

I am in a busy place,
busy place,
busy place,
I am in a busy place,
Where do you think I am?

Can you think of actions to go with this song?

Discussion

Points to bring out

- Some places are busy.
- Busy places are busy because people need or like to go there.

Strategies to try

(*Show items collected from busy places.*) Look at these things I have collected. They all come from places that a lot of people visit. Can you can guess where each thing comes from?

(*Show items again.*) Who has been to the place where this comes from?

What can you tell us about this place? (*Prompt the children – it is a busy place.*)

Why do so many people visit/use these places?

Do people do the same things at all of these places?

What other busy places can we think of?

There are many kinds of busy places. Is a school a busy place?

Look at these places (*Show pictures of factories, offices, etc.*)

What is this place?

What happens here?

Is it a busy place?

Is there anything like it around here?

Follow-up activity

Hand out copies of **The busy place copymaster** and ask the children to make the place in the picture 'busy' by filling it with people.

Game

The children sit in a circle. One child is chosen to skip around the circle while the rest of the children sing the verse from the **Where am I? game**. The child stops skipping when the song ends.

Whoever the child stops behind is then chosen to stand in the circle and mime being in a busy place. (You may want to make a list of suggestions before thw game begins.) When the children have guessed correctly the game continues.

The busy place

Where am I?

(A singing game sung to the tune of "Here we go Round the Mulberry Bush".)

I am in a busy place,
busy place,
busy place,
I am in a busy place,
Where do you think I am?

Can you think of actions to go with this song?

[Affix school letterhead if required]

Dear Parent/Guardian,

Can you help?
In preparation for a lesson we are having it would be very helpful if you could read this letter from your child.

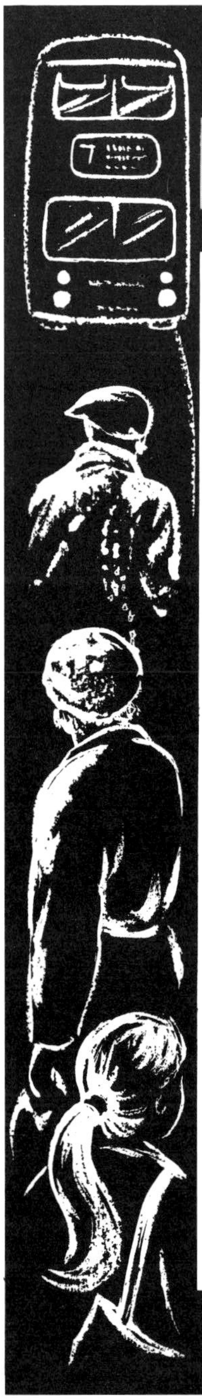

Busy places

In school we are going to have a lesson called "Busy places".

Please could you tell me:

- What is the busiest place you go each week?
- Why do you go there?
- How do you get there?
- Do you enjoy going?
- How long have you been going to this place?
- Do you go with anyone?
- Do you like busy places?
- Are there any busy places you don't like? Why?
- Would you like me to tell you about the busy places I go?

Thank you for helping me,

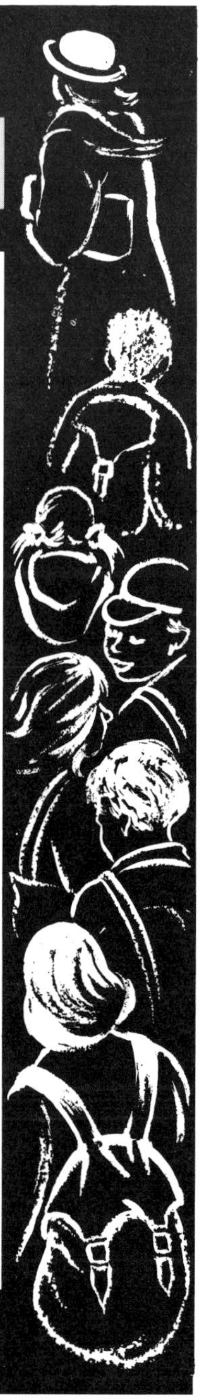

18

Quiet places

THE SOUND ENVIRONMENT

Aims

- to help children understand the importance of 'quiet places'.
- to make children aware of the need to relax, and to teach them how to give others time and space to relax.

Preparation

Choose a quiet venue in the local area (for example, a church, mosque or temple, a library or a park, a woodland walk or quiet seashore, a quiet street). It should be a place to which many people have full access but which is usually quiet. If it is possible arrange a visit to this place. If a visit is not possible. try to arrange for a speaker (e.g. a priest, mullah, rabbi, a librarian or country warden) to come and talk about their 'quiet place'.

Make enough copies of the **Quiet places copymaster** so that all of the children can have one each.

Make copies of the **Meditation copymaster**, as necessary

Discussion

Points to bring out

- There are many quiet places in our community.
- People need quiet places.
- Sometimes it is good to be in a quiet place.

Strategies to try

We are going on a visit/having a visitor. We are going to visit ______________/listen to __________).

Before we start, let's make a list of all the quiet places we know. (*Take suggestions*). [N.B. Work out what quiet means – not silent but not noisy or busy.]

Who likes quiet places? Why?
Is there a quiet place at home?
Is it good to be quiet sometimes?

On our visit/during our talk we will think about these questions:

Why is this place quiet?
Is it nice that it is quiet?
Do people like this place?
Do people like it because it is quiet?

On return to the class/after the talk ask the children:

What did you think about the place we visited/talked about? Why do people need quiet places? (To work in, to relax in, to think in.)

Where are the quiet places in school?

Follow-up activity

Ask the children to colour and then fill in the **Quiet places copymasters**.

Meditation

This is an opportunity to calm children down after a particularly boisterous activity. Ask the children to sit quietly and to read together the verse from the **Meditation copymaster**. When they have said the verse, allow some time to pass. The children must listen for sounds outside the class. Name a child and ask them to say what they can hear. This can be repeated until there are no more sounds to be heard.

Quiet places

Write or draw something to go with these words.

When I am quiet I can:

I like to be quiet when:

What I like best about being quiet is:

MEDITATION

Read this verse:

Quiet, quiet – close your eyes.

Now what can you hear?

Listen, listen – do not speak.

What sounds are there near?

[Affix school letterhead if required]

Just to say a big

THANK YOU

for all the help you have given.

From

FURTHER RESOURCES

***Answers* – A cross-curricular programme for primary schools**
The *Time to Talk* series covers PSHE up to age 7. *Answers*, also published by Collins Educational, covers PSHE for ages 7-11. The series comes in two packs – *Answers Pack 1*, ISBN 000 312006 6, (for ages 7-9) and *Answers Pack 2*, ISBN 000312007 4, (for ages 9-11). Each pack contains a 160-page, photocopiable teachers' book and twenty-four full colour A3 posters.

Collins Educational also publishes a wide range of resources which can be used to support the topics covered in the *Time to Talk* series.

Stories, poems and plays are a particularly effective way of teaching PSHE at this age range. Relevant Collins' titles include:

From the *Book Bus* reading scheme packs –
My Turn, Your Turn; *Henrietta Gets a Blaster* (both dealing with the topic of consideration); *The Enormous Turnip* (team work); *Male and Female* (sex education); *Young and Old* (understanding ageing); *The Boy Who Cried Wolf* (honesty); *Gone for Good* (conservation).

From the Collins *Cascades* series & *Young Lion Storybooks* –
Cynthia Voigt, *A Solitary Blue*, ISBN 000 6726836 (loneliness and family break-up); Judith Kerr, *When Hitler Stole Pink Rabbit*, ISBN 000 6708013 (coping with change); Noel Streatfeild, *The Painted Garden*, ISBN 000 673765X (moving house); Rachel Anderson, *Paper Faces*, ISBN 000 674952X (family relationships); Ann Jungman, *Lucy Keeps the Wolf from the Door*, ISBN 000 6730507 (vegetarianism); Marlene Fanta Shyer, *Welcome Home Jellybean*, ISBN 000 3300188 (dealing with a handicapped child in the family); Gene Kemp, *Just Ferret*, ISBN 000 3300846 (bullying); Berlie Doherty, *Tough Luck*, ISBN 000 3300579 (starting a new school).

From the R.E.A.L. series
The *R.E.A.L* (Religion, Education and Life) *Infant Assembly Book*, ISBN 000 312004 X, includes work which can be linked directly to topics covered in *Time to Talk*. The R.E.A.L storybook *A Tapestry of Tales*, ISBN 000 312000 7, contains numerous moral stories from the six main religions.

If you would like to receive inspection copies of any of these titles, please write to:

Collins Educational, HarperCollins*Publishers*, FREEPOST GW 5078, Bishopbriggs, Glasgow G64 1BR.
Tel: 0141 306 3484. Fax: 0141 306 3750.
